Original title:
When I'm Whole Again

Copyright © 2024 Swan Charm
All rights reserved.

Author: Lan Donne
ISBN HARDBACK: 978-9916-89-604-4
ISBN PAPERBACK: 978-9916-89-605-1
ISBN EBOOK: 978-9916-89-606-8

Unraveling the Past

Threads of time weave tight,
Stories fade in the light,
Memories whisper low,
Secrets only we know.

Each stitch holds a truth,
Binding sorrow and youth,
In shadows, we dwell,
What lessons to tell?

Fragments scattered wide,
In corners, we hide,
Eyes search for a clue,
To who once was you.

Echoes of laughter sound,
In places once profound,
Revisiting each dream,
As if caught in a stream.

The past, a gentle tear,
Both beautiful and sheer,
With hope ahead, we strive,
In memories, we thrive.

A Garden of Lost Dreams

In soil rich and dark,
Whispers of hope embark,
Petals that once bloomed bright,
Now fade into the night.

We water with our tears,
Nurtured by hidden fears,
Each flower holds a tale,
Of journeys that seemed frail.

Twisted vines now creep,
Into memories we keep,
Nature's silent sigh,
Beneath the vast, blue sky.

Soft winds carry the past,
As shadows long are cast,
In this garden we find,
Seek solace intertwined.

Yet from roots deep in pain,
New dreams rise up again,
With every sunlit beam,
We tend to lost dreams' gleam.

The Beauty of Imperfection

A cracked pot in the sun,
Reflects journeys begun,
Flaws that tell a tale,
Of storms that made us pale.

Jagged edges appear,
Yet hold beauty sincere,
In moments left unplanned,
Life's canvas, ungrand.

An uneven path we tread,
With dreams broken, yet spread,
In laughter and in tears,
We embrace our true fears.

The colors may not blend,
Yet they twist and they mend,
In every broken piece,
Lies a chance for release.

So cherish every scar,
They tell us who we are,
In this flawed, perfect dance,
Embrace life's second chance.

Clarity Through Chaos

In swirling thoughts and noise,
I search for hidden poise,
Amongst the wildest storm,
Emerges a quiet form.

Chaos dances around,
But stillness can be found,
In breaths both slow and deep,
Awake from worries' sleep.

Fragments whirl and spin,
Yet peace can dwell within,
In the eye of the storm,
I find a soft, warm charm.

Colors clash and collide,
But I learn to abide,
In the mess, I can see,
A clearer path for me.

Amidst the grand disarray,
Emerges a brighter day,
For in life's wild embrace,
I discover my own grace.

Fragments of a Restored Soul

In shadows deep, the heart once lay,
A broken mirror, hues of gray.
Yet in the cracks, light starts to creep,
Awakening whispers from the deep.

Each shard a story, lost but found,
In silence, echoes all around.
A tapestry of wounds and grace,
Each piece a gift, a sacred space.

The journey forward, one step brave,
Through stormy nights, the soul will save.
For what is lost can still be whole,
Embracing all, a restored soul.

The winds of change begin to sway,
Carrying dreams that won't decay.
Collecting fragments, one by one,
Under the warmth of a rising sun.

With every piece, a lesson learned,\nFires of hope within me burned.
For in the pain, there is a goal,
To find the beauty of the soul.

Picking Up the Pieces

A heart once shattered on the floor,
Now gathers strength from every score.
With trembling hands, I start the task,
To find the jewels behind the mask.

Each fallen piece, a memory sweet,
Reviving lives in rhythmic beat.
Piecing together what once was lost,
In the light of hope, I'll pay the cost.

Resilience blooms in gentle hues,
From ashes rise my vibrant views.
With every shard, a story spun,
Of battles fought and races won.

In tender care, I shape the clay,
Mending hurt in a brand-new way.
Every fragment speaks of grace,
In picking up, I'll find my place.

With patience sown, the heart will heal,
A stronger self, a radiant feel.
In the art of life, I find release,
Picking up pieces, I craft my peace.

Whispers of Renewal

Quiet breaths in the morning light,
Nature's song takes gentle flight.
In each blade of grass, a tale unfolds,
Of whispers soft, of dreams retold.

The dawn arrives, a palette bright,
Colors swirled in pure delight.
Renewal blooms in every heart,
A chance to rise, to play a part.

In silence, echoes form the past,
Lessons learned, forever cast.
Hope unfurls like petals wide,
In whispers soft, I will abide.

With every smile, the world ignites,
A tapestry of shared delights.
Together we embrace the day,
In renewal's glow, we find our way.

So let the whispers guide our souls,
Through winding paths, where beauty rolls.
In the dance of life, we clearly see,
Renewal's song lives within me.

The Symphony of Rebirth

In twilight's glow, the stars align,
A symphony played, a sacred sign.
With every note, a spirit soars,
In the grandeur of life, an open doors.

The past, a melody soft and sweet,
Resonates, as hearts skip a beat.
In harmony, the pain dissolves,
With every chord, a dream evolves.

The rhythm of life, a pulse divine,
Awakening souls, a spark to shine.
In crescendos, we rise and fall,
Together we dance, answering the call.

With winds of change, we learn to fly,
In every challenge, we touch the sky.
Loyal notes mark our path ahead,
In this symphony, worries shed.

As dawn breaks forth with gentle grace,
Rebirth's embrace, a warm embrace.
In unity, we claim our worth,
Creating magic in our rebirth.

Thorns to Petals: A Transformation

From dark and jagged wounds of pain,
New life emerges, blossoms gain.
The thorns that held the heart in place,
Now soften in the sun's embrace.

Each tear that fell upon the ground,
Nurtured roots where hope is found.
Beneath the weight of sorrow's night,
Awakens dreams, ready for flight.

In shadows deep, one learns to fight,
For every thorn, there's pure delight.
To rise from ashes, to be made whole,
To feel the warmth upon the soul.

With petals bright, the past transcends,
Transforming darkness, it mends and bends.
The journey marked by love and grace,
In every bloom, a new embrace.

From thorns to petals, life shall weave,
The tales of strength that hearts believe.
A vibrant dance, a story spun,
In every breath, a chance begun.

The Symphony of Being Whole

Each note we play, a thread in time,
Together weave a life sublime.
In harmony, our spirits rise,
A melody beneath the skies.

The chords of laughter, slight and sweet,
Composed with love, our hearts' heartbeat.
Through trials faced, we learn to sing,
And find the joy that hope can bring.

A symphony of light and shade,
In every moment, music made.
The silence too, a vital part,
In stillness rests the beating heart.

From whispered dreams to roaring cheers,
We harmonize our hopes and fears.
In unity, our voices blend,
A beautiful song that will not end.

Through every chapter, every role,
We play our part, we seek the whole.
Together bound, forever free,
In this grand symphony of being we.

Remnants of a Brighter Tomorrow

Amidst the ruins of today,
Lie seeds of hope, come what may.
In scattered shards, the light will gleam,
A tapestry of a better dream.

Each fragment shines, a gentle guide,
Through darkened paths, it will abide.
The echoes whisper tales of grace,
Of brighter days we shall embrace.

From ashes cold, a fire ignites,
With every struggle, spirit fights.
Together stealing a glance ahead,
In every heartbeat, love is spread.

Remnants tell of trails once trod,
Of lessons learned beneath the sod.
In every scar, a story's claim,
Of courage forged through love's own flame.

A future bright, we hold in hand,
Together we, a stronger band.
With remnants cherished, hearts shall soar,
For brighter tomorrows, we explore.

In Search of the Lost Threads

Once woven tight, the fabric frays,
Through tangled paths, we roam, we sway.
In search of threads that slip away,
To bind the moments, here we stay.

The colors fade, yet visions hold,
A tapestry of stories told.
In whispers light, the truth we seek,
The fragile spots, the strong, the weak.

We comb the past for golden strands,
Embrace the touch of loving hands.
Reviving dreams that time forgot,
In every stitch, a battle fought.

The threads of laughter, tears, and time,
Together form a life, sublime.
A quest for wholeness, hearts extend,
In search of threads that never end.

For in this quest, we learn and grow,
Each lost thread brings a brighter glow.
We reweave fate, our hands so bold,
In search of threads, our stories told.

Love's Return to the Heart

In quiet corners, shadows play,
Once lost affection finds its way.
The whispers soft, like gentle sighs,
And in their warmth, the spirit flies.

Embers of laughter spark anew,
Where darkness faded, light breaks through.
In tender moments, souls align,
A dance of hearts, both yours and mine.

Through trials faced, we've gleaned the truth,
In every bruise, a spark of youth.
The past, a maze, now paved with care,
Through every turn, love leads us there.

With open arms, we face the dawn,
Each shared dream a promise drawn.
Together forged, we rise and soar,
In love's embrace, forevermore.

The Wind Chime of New Beginnings

A gentle breeze stirs soft and clear,
The wind chime sings, the world draws near.
Each note a promise, bright and bold,
Awakening stories yet untold.

Sunrise glimmers on the horizon,
New paths unfold, like whispers risen.
With every sound, hope starts to bloom,
In fragile hearts, dispelling gloom.

Change dances lightly, yet profound,
In every heartbeat, love is found.
And from the silence, courage flows,
In this bouquet, the spirit grows.

So take a step, embrace the song,
In life's great symphony, we belong.
Together, we'll weave this tapestry,
With threads of joy, and harmony.

Echoes of Healing

Beneath the layers, scars still speak,
In whispered tales, the journey's streak.
With tender hands, we stitch the seams,
As hope ignites our buried dreams.

Time's gentle touch begins to mend,
In every heart, a faithful friend.
Fragments glimmer, reflecting light,
In darkest hours, we reclaim our sight.

Each tear released, a drop of grace,
In solace found, we find our place.
A symphony of strength resounds,
In love and kindness, healing bounds.

From shadowed pasts, we rise anew,
In every heartbeat, courage grew.
Together bound, we'll stand and breathe,
In echoes sweet, our hearts believe.

In the Stillness of Reassembly

In quiet moments, pieces fall,
A puzzle's grace, embracing all.
With every breath, we start to see,
The beauty lies in what can be.

Fragments move, dance to the light,
Transforming shadow into sight.
With open hearts, we find the way,
To stitch together night and day.

Through silent prayer, intentions rise,
In stillness found, our spirits fly.
A canvas blank, we paint anew,
With shades of courage, bold and true.

In gentle rhythms, life takes form,
Amidst the chaos, we are warm.
As hands unite, and dreams align,
In love's embrace, we intertwine.

Mending the Tapestry of Being

Threads of colors intertwine,
In the fabric of our soul.
Worn but rich with stories,
Each stitch makes us whole.

Scars that tell of battles fought,
Embrace the light they bring.
With every tear we learn to weave,
A deeper, stronger string.

Patterns shift with time's soft hand,
Life's dance, both fierce and sweet.
We gather up the broken links,
To form a tapestry neat.

Through laughter and through tears we find,
The beauty in the fray.
Together, in this sacred space,
We choose to not betray.

In mending what was once undone,
We find our truest self.
A tapestry of love and hope,
We hang upon a shelf.

Whispers of a Unified Spirit

In silence, minds can meet,
A gentle hum of peace.
Spirits merge in quiet thought,
Together, we release.

Each whisper shared defies the dark,
A bond that softly glows.
Connection found in simple joys,
A light that ever flows.

Through shadows and through light we walk,
Hands clasped in unity.
In every breath, the world's embrace,
A dance of harmony.

Voices blend like honey sweet,
With kindness, hearts align.
The whispers of our unified souls,
Compose a grand design.

In every challenge, every dream,
Together, we stand tall.
The whispers guide us, hand in hand,
Boundless, we can't fall.

Reflections in a Shattered Mirror

Each shard tells a tale untold,
Fragments caught in time.
Reflections dance in broken light,
A fleeting, fractured rhyme.

In chaos, patterns start to form,
A glimpse of what may be.
Through jagged glass, a truth reveals,
A self we'd yet to see.

We gather pieces, one by one,
Beneath the weight of dreams.
In the cracks, new visions bloom,
Woven by hopeful themes.

From splintered visions, strength emerges,
Each cut sings of desire.
Through acceptance, we embrace the scars,
Transforming pain to fire.

In reflecting on the shattered past,
We find a way to mend.
Through every break, we rise anew,
A journey without end.

The Art of Becoming Whole

In every fragment lies a gem,
Waiting for the light.
We gather what we thought was lost,
To create the perfect sight.

Steps may falter, hearts may ache,
Yet wisdom gently grows.
In every stumble, there's a grace,
A seed that softly sows.

With patience, we embrace the cracks,
That tell our story true.
In every flaw, a beauty waits,
To guide us through the blue.

The art of being whole demands,
An openness to change.
To weave our threads of joy and pain,
In patterns that arrange.

Through open hearts and joining hands,
We manifest our dreams.
In the dance of life, we're never lost,
Together, we are beams.

Finding Beauty in the Brokenness

In cracks of life, light seeps through,
A mosaic of scars, stories anew.
Each piece whispers of battles fought,
In brokenness, beauty is wrought.

Shattered hearts find a unique song,
In the chaos, we learn we belong.
With every fracture, strength appears,
A tapestry woven through our tears.

Embrace the flaws, let shadows dance,
In the imperfect, we find our chance.
A journey shaped by love's embrace,
In brokenness, we find our place.

No longer hiding, we stand in grace,
In the light of truth, we find our space.
Beauty blooms where hopes have soared,
In every crack, our souls are restored.

So let the brokenness shine bright,
In its embrace, we find our light.
With every scar, we rise and grow,
In finding beauty, our spirits glow.

The Infinite Path to Wholeness

Step by step, we walk the line,
Through valleys deep, our hearts entwine.
Each moment teaches us to see,
The wholeness found within the free.

Branches reach for the sunlit sky,
As shadows fall, we learn to fly.
In every stumble, lessons come,
In every heartbeat, we feel home.

The winds of change whisper our names,
In the dance of life, we play our games.
With open hearts, we face the storm,
In unity's grace, our spirits warm.

Every step, a sacred prayer,
A journey taken, we lay it bare.
Through twists and turns, we find our way,
In the infinite, we learn to stay.

So trust the path that unfolds still,
With every breath, embrace the will.
In wholeness, we discover the song,
In every step, we find where we belong.

Soul's Journey Towards Integration

In the silence, the soul does speak,
As fragments yearn for the unity they seek.
Every shadow, every light,
Is a whisper guiding us through the night.

With every layer, we peel away,
A deeper truth begins to sway.
In the dance of light and dark,
Integration ignites the spark.

Moments linger, lessons learned,
In the heart's fire, passion burned.
Embrace the whole, the parts combined,
In unity, our spirits aligned.

Each step leads closer to the core,
Where love resides, forevermore.
Through the journey, we come to know,
Integration helps our true selves grow.

So walk the path with open eyes,
Embrace the highs, the lows, the cries.
In the journey, the soul finds its peace,
In integration, we find release.

Colors of the Soul Redeemed

A canvas wide, colors unfold,
In shades of sorrow, glimmers of gold.
Each hue tells a story untold,
In the depths of the heart, we are bold.

Crimson dreams mixed with azure night,
Every stroke brings a heart's delight.
In the palette of life's embrace,
We find redemption in love's grace.

Emerald hopes, and maroon fears,
Brush against the laughter and tears.
In every color, the soul ignites,
Painting a world that reflects our fights.

Through the storms, a vibrant theme,
In the chaos, we learn to dream.
With open hearts, we dare to see,
The soul's colors, wild and free.

So let us cherish each faded shade,
In every tone, a bond we've made.
In the colors of the soul, we find,
A tapestry woven, lovingly entwined.

Songs of the Unbroken Spirit

In shadows deep, we find our light,
Resilience blooms, a wondrous sight.
With every tear that falls like rain,
We rise again, we break the chain.

Voices echo, strong and clear,
The songs of hope, we hold so dear.
In unity, our spirits soar,
Together we can be much more.

Mountains stand, but hearts are bold,
With every story, courage told.
Our dreams ignite, a vibrant thread,
In every heartbeat, life is spread.

Through trials faced, we will not yield,
Our strength revealed, our fate is sealed.
A tapestry of scars and grace,
The unbroken spirit we embrace.

So raise your voice, let laughter free,
In every note, the soul's decree.
We are the ones who will inspire,
With songs that lift, set hearts on fire.

Touching the Depths of Restoration

In the silence, wounds will mend,
A whispered touch, the heart can send.
In gentle waves, the past meets peace,
A moment's grace, a sweet release.

The roots run deep, the soil turns gold,
From ashes rise, stories unfold.
With every heartbeat, spirit glows,
A dance of life, the river flows.

Through darkest nights, a star will shine,
In the depths, we learn to climb.
A journey vast, yet felt so near,
Together we will conquer fear.

From shattered dreams, new visions spark,
In whispered hopes, we find our mark.
Each fragment lifts, a sacred grace,
Restoration's warmth in every space.

With open arms, the dawn will break,
In stillness found, the heart will wake.
We find our way, the path is clear,
In depths of love, we persevere.

A Heart Reconstructed

Once broken down, now rising high,
Each sturdy piece, a reason why.
In whispered thoughts, and love's embrace,
A heart reconstructed finds its place.

Amidst the rubble, light will stream,
From shattered vows, we dare to dream.
With every scar, a story's grace,
In every trial, the soul's bright face.

The courage grows with every beat,
In darkened paths, we find our feet.
With hope aligned, the soul restored,
Each moment cherished, love adored.

From fractured dreams, new patterns weave,
A symphony of hearts that believe.
In lifetimes past, the lessons gleaned,
A heart reborn, forever dreamed.

So take a step, embrace the change,
The journey's curve may feel so strange.
Yet in this space, we rise anew,
With every breath, a joy made true.

The Flame of Rebirth

In ashes cold, a spark ignites,
The flame of hope in darkest nights.
From ember's glow, new life begins,
The dance of joy in gentle spins.

With every flicker, courage grows,
In shadows deep, the light still glows.
Each moment forged in fire's embrace,
A testament to time and space.

The heart awakes, a phoenix rise,
In golden hues, beneath the skies.
Through trials faced, we forge our fate,
In flames of love, we celebrate.

From fragile threads, we weave so bright,
A tapestry of pure delight.
With strength renewed, we journey forth,
The flame of rebirth gives us worth.

So gather round, let stories soar,
In every heart, there's room for more.
With open arms, we spark the fire,
In each rebirth, we find our desire.

A Canvas Repainted

Colors blend in vibrant hues,
A story told in every bruise.
Brush of fate, in hands so bold,
A masterpiece from shards of gold.

From shadows deep, light starts to gleam,
Each layer adds to the dream.
Textures rich, with tales to share,
Each stroke whispers of the care.

The heart beats loud, the canvas sings,
Hope, like a kite, takes to the wings.
In every fold, a life reborn,
New visions rise with each new dawn.

Past pain washed with gentle grace,
Beauty found in every trace.
With every flick, the spirit free,
A world awaits, just wait and see.

As colors dance and spirits rise,
A canvas crafted 'neath the skies.
With bold intent, the palette swirls,
In art, we find our inner worlds.

Resilience in the Face of Fracture

Cracks appear, but do not break,
Strength emerges from the ache.
With every dent, a story speaks,
Resilience thrives, the heart still seeks.

Like ancient trees that bend but stand,
Roots go deep in troubled land.
Through storms that howl and winds that bite,
A spirit forged in darkest night.

When shadows loom and hope seems lost,
We count the courage, not the cost.
With every scar, a badge of fight,
Resilience blooms, a guiding light.

In fractures wide, new paths are born,
From shattered dreams, a future's dawn.
With strength anew, we rise from tears,
Embracing change, shedding our fears.

So when the world feels cold and gray,
Remember, dawn will find the way.
In fractures deep, we learn to stand,
Resilience binds us, hand in hand.

Rising from the Ashes of Self

In smoky trails, the embers glow,
From loss, a newer self will grow.
With every flame that used to burn,
A phoenix waits for its return.

With ashes clinging to the ground,
A hidden strength can still be found.
In quiet moments, whispers say,
You are reborn, don't fade away.

The past may haunt with shadows past,
But futures bright are meant to last.
With wings spread wide, the heart ignites,
On paths untraveled, courage bites.

There lies within a spark divine,
In rising up, the soul will shine.
So take the leap, embrace the fire,
From ashes, birth your true desire.

In every end, begins the start,
Hope's gentle flame will warm the heart.
So rise again, let courage swell,
Be the hero in your tale to tell.

The Dance of the Integrated Soul

In harmony, the spirit sways,
Lost in the music of our days.
Each step a note, in rhythm found,
In stillness deep, we dance around.

With whispers soft, the heart takes flight,
In shadows cast, we find the light.
With every twirl, the pieces blend,
An integrated journey, not an end.

The tapestry of thought and breath,
In cosmic embrace, we find no death.
With courage held, the spirit spins,
A dance of unity, where love begins.

In silence shared, the soul unfolds,
In every story, a truth untold.
Together we leap, together we fall,
In the dance of life, we find our all.

So let us whirl through night and day,
With open hearts, we find our way.
In every beat, the beauty grows,
The dance of souls, a river flows.

Gathering the Shattered Stars

In the night, pieces glimmer,
Fallen dreams, a cosmic shimmer.
With gentle hands, we find their light,
Mending darkness, crafting bright.

Whispers of hope fill the air,
Every shard, a silent prayer.
Together we weave the scattered glow,
A tapestry of love to show.

Each star tells a story deep,
Secrets kept, in silence, sleep.
We gather them, one by one,
Under the vast and watchful sun.

In the sky, they start to dance,
A symphony of fate and chance.
Aligning hearts, igniting fire,
From shattered selves, we rise, aspire.

So let us lift the broken bright,
Gathering stars, igniting night.
In unity, we find our way,
Transforming night into the day.

Serenity in the Embrace of Wholeness

In quiet corners, peace descends,
A gentle touch that softly mends.
Embracing truths, we breathe, we grow,
In this moment, let love flow.

The world outside fades to a hum,
In wholeness found, we softly come.
Warmth of solace wraps us tight,
Guiding hearts through the gentle night.

Within this space, all fears dissolve,
In harmony, we find resolve.
Wholeness sings, a tender song,
In collective arms, we belong.

Silence whispers of what is real,
In every heartbeat, we can feel.
A sanctuary where souls align,
Finding unity, yours and mine.

So let us rest, let burdens cease,
In this embrace, we find our peace.
Serenity flows, a gentle tide,
Together we stand, side by side.

Wholeness in the Quiet Moments

In the silence, whispers wane,
Echoing softly like gentle rain.
Hearts entwined in stillness share,
The beauty found when we lay bare.

Breath by breath, we weave and mend,
Every pause, a sacred blend.
In quietude, our spirits rise,
As truth unfolds before our eyes.

Soft shadows dance in twilight's glow,
In stillness, seeds of love we sow.
Moments woven, threads of gold,
In the quiet, stories told.

Calmness lingers, like a sigh,
Beneath the vast, embracing sky.
In every heartbeat, we discern,
The lessons that the stillness earns.

So let us cherish what we find,
In quiet moments, hearts aligned.
Wholeness blooms as silence reigns,
And love's embrace forever gains.

The Palette of a Unified Heart

Colors blend in shades so bright,
A canvas painted with pure light.
Each stroke tells a tale of grace,
In every hue, we find our place.

Unity dances in bold arrays,
Threads of love sewn through our days.
With every heartbeat, colors spin,
In the spectrum where we begin.

Violet whispers, sapphire dreams,
Emerald hopes beneath the beams.
In the warmth of a unified art,
Lies the beauty of the heart.

Together we craft a vivid scene,
Where every moment's rich and keen.
In the palette, shades of being,
Life's masterpiece, forever freeing.

So let us paint with all we are,
A tapestry, our guiding star.
In the colors of love, we stand,
Unified, hand in hand.

In the Embrace of Completion

As the sun sets, shadows dance,
Life's chapters end, a sweet romance.
Bridges burned, yet lessons learned,
In the embrace, our souls yearn.

Gratitude flows like a gentle stream,
Whispers of hope in every dream.
With open hearts, we bid goodbye,
Completion sings, a soft sigh.

Each moment cherished, a fleeting glance,
In stillness, we find our chance.
Completed paths weave stories true,
In the embrace, it's me and you.

The stars align, a cosmic thread,
Binding all the words unsaid.
Finding peace in the twilight's glow,
In completion's arms, we let go.

Together we rise, renewed in grace,
In the embrace of this sacred space.
Completion whispers, we are one,
In this journey, the heart has won.

Echoes of a Unified Heart

In quiet whispers, our souls convene,
Boundless love in the spaces unseen.
Harmony flows like a gentle tide,
In echoes of hearts, we confide.

Resonance strong, our spirits dance,
In every glance, we find our chance.
A melody sweet, woven in time,
Unified hearts in rhythm, sublime.

Across the valleys, through the night,
Each heartbeat calls, a guiding light.
Together we rise, hand in hand,
In echoes of love, we understand.

The world may tremble, storms may rage,
Yet here we stand, turning the page.
In unity we find our way,
Echoes of a heart, come what may.

With each embrace, our fears subside,
In the symphony, we take pride.
United whispers fill the air,
Echoes linger, love laid bare.

Reclaiming My Essence

In the stillness, shadows fade,
Fragments lost, but not betrayed.
With every breath, I reclaim me,
In the depths, I set my spirit free.

The mirror reflects a familiar face,
Through the chaos, I find my place.
Peeling layers, embracing truth,
Reclaiming the fire of my youth.

Voices muted, now I stand tall,
Breaking free from the binding thrall.
With gentle strength, I rise and soar,
Reclaiming my essence, forevermore.

Through trials faced and rivers crossed,
In every heartbeat, nothing's lost.
Resilience blooms like a flower bold,
In reclaiming, I see my soul unfold.

The journey inward is never vain,
Through the darkness, I embrace the pain.
Reclaiming my truth, I find my way,
In this essence, I choose to stay.

The Journey to Wholeness

Step by step, I walk the line,
Each footfall sings, the stars align.
With purpose clear and vision bright,
The journey calls into the night.

Mountains high, valleys wide,
Inside me dwells a world of pride.
With every challenge, I become whole,
The journey weaves into my soul.

Through storms I face, through trials faced,
In every heartache, love is placed.
The road may twist, the path may bend,
But in every turn, I will transcend.

With open arms, I greet the dawn,
A tapestry of life is drawn.
Wholeness beckons, a gentle breeze,
The journey leads where the spirit frees.

Each destination, a new embrace,
Finding joy in the sacred space.
The journey teaches, I am enough,
In the quest for wholeness, I find love.

Journey Through Unraveled Threads

In tangled strands, my thoughts reside,
Winding paths where dreams collide.
Each twist a turn, each knot a tale,
Through shadows deep, I find my trail.

With every step, I pull the seam,
Unraveling fears, igniting dreams.
Light breaks through the woven cloth,
A tapestry of what I'm not.

The journey pulls me from the dark,
A flicker born from each new spark.
I stitch the edges, mend the fray,
Finding strength in threads of gray.

Woven memories, sweet and sour,
With each connection, I gain power.
In every loop, a lesson learned,
Through fragile threads, my spirit burned.

I weave my story, bold and bright,
In the dance of day and night.
Through these threads, the world I see,
A journey forged, I set it free.

Finding Harmony in Disarray

Amid the chaos, a whisper sings,
In tangled notes where discord clings.
Yet in the mess, I start to find,
The rhythm flows within the blind.

Fragments scattered, paths that sway,
In the storm, I make my way.
Each note a step, each fault a chance,
To join the wild, imperfect dance.

Voices clashing, yet they blend,
A melody born where rules suspend.
In disarray, I find my ground,
The sweetest notes in chaos found.

With open hearts, we learn to see,
The beauty formed through discord's plea.
In tangled days and nights in sway,
Harmony waits in disarray.

So let the storm rage on and roar,
Within the mess, I'll seek for more.
For in each struggle, life's a song,
Finding sweet harmony where I belong.

The Restoration of Light Within

In twilight's grasp, a flicker glows,
A yearning heart that gently knows.
Through shadows deep, a spark remains,
In quiet moments, light reclaims.

Restoration starts with breaths so slow,
As dawn's embrace begins to show.
With every pulse, the warmth ignites,
Transforming dark into vibrant sights.

Within the silence, whispers rise,
A journey back to clearer skies.
The pieces fall, aligned with grace,
Reflecting truth in every place.

With broken parts, I learn to mend,
Embracing flaws as faithful friends.
The light within, a guiding star,
Shows me just how bright we are.

So let me wander, seek, and learn,
For every bruise, a chance to yearn.
Restoration blooms in every heart,
A tender light, a work of art.

Pieces to the Puzzle of Me

Scattered fragments on the floor,
Each a hint of who I am, more.
The puzzle waits, a dance of fate,
To fit these bits, I patiently wait.

Colors mingle, shapes align,
In every piece, a story's sign.
Through prismatic shades, I start to see,
The intricate mosaic of me.

With every fit, I breathe anew,
A canvas painted in vibrant hue.
In gaps of blue and bursts of red,
I find the words I've left unsaid.

The corners hold my darkest nights,
While edges gleam with hopeful lights.
Each section speaks of trials past,
Creating wholeness, built to last.

So here I stand, a piece complete,
In this puzzle, life so sweet.
With every fragment, I embrace
The beauty found in my own space.

The Ascendance of the Soul

In the quiet dawn, spirits arise,
Chasing shadows, they touch the skies.
With whispers soft, they find their way,
To realms where light begins to play.

Through trials fierce, they learn to fly,
Unfolding wings, they seek the high.
Each heartbeat draws them close to grace,
A gentle dance in sacred space.

Beneath the stars, their promise glows,
In the night, a new life grows.
With faith as strong as ancient stone,
The soul, at last, is not alone.

Through winding paths, they wander free,
Unraveling truths, they learn to see.
A symphony of dreams unspun,
In unity, they now are one.

Reweaving the Fabric of Existence

Threads of gold in the loom of time,
Stitching moments, they dance in rhyme.
With intentions pure, they weave a tale,
Binding hearts and letting spirits sail.

In colors bright, they paint the night,
With hopes and sorrows, shadows take flight.
Each knot a lesson, each twist a chance,
To find connection in the cosmic dance.

From fibers frayed, new patterns rise,
In the tapestry, we glimpse the wise.
A gentle hum of life's embrace,
In the woven threads, we find our place.

With every stitch, we share the glow,
Tales of love and loss we sow.
In unity, the fabric grows,
Reflecting all that nature knows.

Blossoming in the Wake of Healing

In gentle rains, the flowers bloom,
Emerging from the depths of gloom.
With petals soft, they greet the sun,
In the warmth of love, they've just begun.

Through storms endured, they find their way,
With roots of strength, they choose to stay.
Each drop of dew, a story told,
In every hue, their hearts unfold.

The fragrance sweet, a fragrant past,
In healing light, their shadows cast.
With every breath, a promise made,
In the wake of pain, hope won't fade.

Beneath the sky, they sway and dance,
Embracing life, a second chance.
In the garden of time, they rejoice,
A chorus of life, they lift their voice.

Embracing the Whirlwind of Becoming

In the eye of storm, we learn to stand,
With open hearts, we take life's hand.
In swirling winds, our spirits rise,
With courage fierce, we touch the skies.

Through chaos soft, we find our ground,
In the dance of life, the lost are found.
Each turn reveals a hidden grace,
In every challenge, a new embrace.

With every gust, our souls ignite,
Transforming darkness into light.
The journey long, yet worth the fight,
In the whirlwind's heart, we find our might.

As seasons shift, we learn to flow,
In every twist, we come to know.
Embracing change as part of us,
In becoming whole, we learn to trust.

Rewriting My Story

In shadows where I used to hide,
I find the light that helps me grow.
With every word, I break the tide,
New chapters bloom, new colors show.

The ink now flows with hope and grace,
A pen in hand, I claim my right.
To reshape dreams in a new space,
And chase the stars, igniting night.

With courage, I unbind my truth,
The past, a whisper, fades away.
Each line I write, a spark of youth,
A bold new dawn, a bright array.

I'll craft a tale of strength and pride,
With love as ink, my heart as page.
In every twist, I choose to bide,
The story's mine; I set the stage.

No longer lost, I blaze my trail,
Embracing fate with open arms.
In every fail, there's growth to hail,
My heart now sings, my spirit charms.

Harmony in Dissonance

In tangled notes a beauty lies,
A melody that twists and turns.
Through all the chaos, courage flies,
Where every clash a lesson earns.

The heartbeat of our souls entwined,
In every step, a dance we make.
With every struggle, love defined,
Through disarray, new paths we take.

The echoes of our doubts arise,
Yet still, we find a rhythm sweet.
We chase the dreams that fill the skies,
In perfect time, our hearts compete.

Resilience found in close embrace,
Through ups and downs, we interlace.
As thunder roars, we softly sing,
In every storm, our souls take wing.

Together, we will face the night,
With fractured chords, we craft our tune.
In harmony, we find the light,
A symphony beneath the moon.

The Road to Reconciliation

Along a path where echoes dwell,
I walk with scars of battles fought.
Each step I take, a wish to quell,
The ghosts of pain, the lessons taught.

Forgiveness blooms in tender grace,
As bridges form across the fray.
With every stride, I find my place,
In unity, old wounds give way.

Conversations born of honesty,
Unravel tales of hurt and shame.
In tears, we plant the seeds of peace,
And kindle hope, a vibrant flame.

We gather strength from shared embrace,
In vulnerability we stand.
The healing heart, a sacred space,
Together, we will build anew, hand in hand.

Each moment now a chance to grow,
To turn the past into a guide.
The road to love is hard, we know,
Yet on this journey, we confide.

Breathing in Belonging

In gentle whispers, roots entwine,
A sacred bond beneath the skin.
With every breath, the stars align,
In every soul, we find our kin.

The warmth of hands, a kindred touch,
We weave our stories, thread by thread.
Through laughter shared, we learn so much,
In unity, the fears we shed.

In open hearts, acceptance glows,
Where differences become our strength.
Together, through the ebb and flows,
In harmony, we grow in length.

With every sunrise, dreams take flight,
In every heartbeat, love's refrain.
The beauty found in shared delight,
A tapestry, not born in vain.

So let us breathe as one tonight,
With open arms, we claim our space.
In all our colors, we ignite,
A world of love, a warm embrace.

The Alchemy of Self-Recovery

In the shadows, I find my spark,
Transforming pain into a work of art.
Each bruise a lesson, each tear a note,
Crafting gold from the heart of the dark.

Embrace the silence, let it teach,
Whispers of healing softly reach.
With every breath, I reclaim my voice,
In the echoes, I find strength to breach.

Amidst the chaos, I stand tall,
Sifting through the ashes, I will not fall.
Resilience blooms in the space of loss,
Together, I rise, I heed the call.

Scars tell stories, etched in time,
Turning wounds into rhymes sublime.
With courage as ink, I write my tale,
In the chapter of self, I learn to climb.

This journey unfolds, a sacred dance,
Bringing fragments together, a chance.
Transforming shadows into bright delight,
In the alchemy of self, I advance.

The Radiance of a Unified Spirit

We are stars sewn in the same sky,
Flickering gently as we draw nigh.
In the warmth of laughter, we intertwine,
Creating constellations that soar high.

Threads of light weave through our hearts,
Binding us closer, never apart.
In this tapestry of love and grace,
Every stitch, a touch of art.

Harmony flows through our collective soul,
Each voice a note, making us whole.
Together we sing, a symphonic wave,
In the melody of life, we find our role.

With every step, we shine anew,
In unity's glow, there's nothing we can't do.
Embracing the differences that we share,
In the radiance of love, we break through.

So let us dance in this cosmic light,
Together we rise, igniting the night.
With hearts aligned, a beautiful sight,
In the symphony of spirits, pure delight.

Interwoven Threads of My Being

In the fabric of my life, I see,
Colors blending, a vivid tapestry.
Each thread a story, each knot a dream,
Together they weave my identity.

From past to present, threads intertwine,
Fading moments, gentle yet divine.
With every experience, I find my way,
In the loom of time, a design so fine.

Emotions ebb and flow, like the tide,
Crafting the patterns where I confide.
In vulnerability, strength is born,
A fabric of love where I abide.

Each stitch a reminder of the journey made,
In the art of living, I am unafraid.
For in every fray lies a chance to heal,
In the interwoven threads, I'll never fade.

So here I stand, clothed in my light,
Embracing the shadows that shape my flight.
In the tapestry of life, wide and vast,
I celebrate my being, both day and night.

Clarity Through the Lens of Healing

In a world of chaos, I seek to see,
Through the fog where shadows flee.
With every breath, I find my ground,
In the clarity of healing, I am free.

Moments of stillness bring insight bright,
Guiding me gently into the light.
Each layer peeled reveals the core,
Through the lens of truth, I ignite.

Grief transforms into wisdom's embrace,
As I navigate this sacred space.
With open heart, I release the past,
Finding peace in my own pace.

Rivers of emotion flow and recede,
Nourishing the roots of my internal seed.
In the landscape of healing, I bloom anew,
With clarity gained, I tend my creed.

With every revelation, I rise and stand,
Embracing the lessons that life has planned.
In the brilliance of healing, I find my way,
Through the lens of clarity, I make my brand.

A Symphony of Completeness

In the quiet dawn, notes softly arise,
Melodies of life beneath sprawling skies.
Each note a moment, uniquely we find,
Harmony whispers, embracing the mind.

With every heartbeat, a rhythm takes flight,
Filling the spaces, transforming the night.
A symphony woven, where souls intertwine,
Creating a chorus, both tender and fine.

In laughter and sorrow, the tune carries on,
Resonant echoes that linger at dawn.
Together we dance, in this vast living sea,
A symphony written, just you and just me.

The strings of our hearts play in perfect time,
Notes merging softly, a subtle climb.
When silence would linger, our voices still sing,
Crafting the music of everything.

Let's cherish these moments, let them unfold,
In this grand orchestra, our stories are told.
Each note a reminder of life's sweet embrace,
A symphony echoing through time and through space.

Heartstrings Rewoven

Threads of emotion, woven with care,
We mend and we stitch, love's delicate wear.
In the laughter and tears, our hearts intertwine,
Crafting a tapestry, both yours and mine.

With each gentle pull, stories unfold,
Colors of passion and memories bold.
From frays and from scars, new patterns emerge,
A dance of resilience, our spirits converge.

The fabric of trust, so tender and bright,
Illuminates paths in the depth of the night.
In shadows we find, the strength to believe,
Together we flourish, together we weave.

As seasons do change, the thread may grow thin,
Yet love is the needle, forever within.
Through storms and through calm, the stitches hold fast,
A promise of beauty, a bond meant to last.

So here's to the journey, the weaving we share,
The heartstrings re-knit, our spirits laid bare.
Each moment a stitch in this masterpiece made,
A tapestry glowing, where love won't fade.

Echoes of the Restored Self

In the silence, whispers find their way,
Soft echoes of hope in the light of the day.
Fragments now gathered, a portrait reclaimed,
The essence of self, both cherished and named.

Through shadows we wander, forgotten and lost,
Braving the storms, embracing the cost.
Each echo a lesson, a story retold,
Reviving the spirit, with courage bold.

The tapestry woven of trials and grace,
Reflecting the strength in the heart's tender space.
In moments of stillness, our truths come alive,
Echoes of promise, where we can survive.

Step by step onward, this journey's begun,
Finding our voices, bright as the sun.
In the dance of remembrance, we rise and we dwell,
In echoes of self, we find who we are well.

With each soft reminder, the spirit restores,
Embracing our whole with wide-open doors.
To love with abandon, with grace and with zeal,
In echoes of self, we discover what's real.

Journey to the Center of Me

A path less traveled, where shadows reside,
To the heart of my being, I wander inside.
With courage as compass, and dreams as my guide,
I journey to places where secrets abide.

Through valleys of doubt, and mountains of hope,
I navigate waters where currents may mope.
Each step is a lesson, a whisper of truth,
The essence of growing and reclaiming my youth.

With each twist and turn, I uncover my soul,
The gem that I cherish, the story I'm whole.
Beneath all the layers, confusion starts to fade,
Revealing the wisdom that time has conveyed.

In the silence I find the rhythm of heart,
The voice of my spirit, an exquisite art.
In stillness, I gather the fragments of me,
Illuminated softly by the light I can see.

So let this journey be sacred and true,
To the center of me and the colors I drew.
In every awakening, I stand and I free,
The treasure of being, the journey of me.

Threads of Healing

In the quiet hum of night,
Gentle whispers in the air,
Stitching wounds with tender light,
Weaving hope with loving care.

Time, a river soft and wide,
Carries sorrows down the stream,
With each ebb, I choose to ride,
Embracing now, a brighter dream.

Nature's balm upon my skin,
Every breath, a brand new start,
Learning to let love seep in,
Mending fractures in my heart.

With each thread I weave anew,
Patterns form in vibrant hues,
A tapestry of what is true,
In this art, my spirit finds clues.

Healing comes in silent streams,
Glistening beneath the stars,
In the dance of fading dreams,
I reclaim what was once ours.

A Mosaic of Me

Fragments scattered in the night,
Pieces of my story gleam,
Each shard reflects a different light,
Together, they form a dream.

Colors clash and softly blend,
Shadows play upon the floor,
Every flaw a special friend,
In this chaos, I find more.

Tiny bits of pain and joy,
Crafted moments, stitched with care,
Life's a game without a toy,
Still, I find beauty everywhere.

Here I stand, a work in progress,
Layers deep with tales untold,
Embracing love, shedding stress,
In this mosaic, I am bold.

Each small piece a journey made,
Through the high and through the low,
In this art, my heart displayed,
A vibrant soul ready to grow.

Dancing with Shadows

In the twilight's soft embrace,
Shadows stretch and softly sway,
Underneath the moon's kind face,
They invite me out to play.

Footsteps echo, swift and light,
Whispers linger in the dark,
I twirl beneath the shimmering night,
Each shadow sparks a hidden spark.

With each step, fear slips away,
The darkness reveals its grace,
In the rhythm, moments sway,
Where shadows dance, I find my place.

Holding hands with fears once known,
I learn to move and glide along,
In the quiet, strength I've grown,
Here in silence, I belong.

Dancing forth, I feel the pull,
Of light and dark, a gentle thread,
In this blend, my heart is full,
With shadows, joy and peace are wed.

The Light Between Cracks

In the silence of the morn,
Light spills through the broken seams,
From the darkness, I am born,
Chasing down the flickered dreams.

Each crack holds a secret glow,
A reminder in the night,
Through the gaps, new hopes will flow,
Finding warmth in every plight.

Nature weaves her softest rays,
Touching hearts that have felt pain,
In the stillness, warmth displays,
Life emerges, like gentle rain.

With each beam that breaks the stone,
Healing starts from what we lack,
In the quiet, I have grown,
Finding strength in every crack.

Light ignites a path so bright,
Guiding souls through perfect flaws,
In the dark, I find my light,
Embracing life with open jaws.

Navigating the Waters of Wholeness

In the depths of midnight seas,
I sail on waves of gentle breeze.
Each ripple tells a story vast,
Of shadows long and light amassed.

To find the shores where silence breathes,
And gather strength from whispered leaves.
The compass points to heart's embrace,
Where every journey finds its place.

I navigate through stormy nights,
Embracing both the dark and lights.
With every swell, I learn to trust,
And turn my fears to grains of dust.

The ocean sings of unity,
In tides of soft immunity.
From fragments lost, I rise anew,
A vessel whole in skies so blue.

A path of stars beneath my wake,
A map of dreams that I shall make.
In every wave, a chance to be,
The sailor of my destiny.

A Dance of Fractured Light

In prisms where the shadows play,
Fragments shift and twirl away.
The echoes of a silent song,
Guide the heart where dreams belong.

Each ray a whisper, soft and bright,
A ballet spun from fractured light.
Amidst the chaos, beauty glows,
As every shard a story sows.

I waltz on edges, sharp yet clear,
Embracing hope, dissolving fear.
In every turn, a spark ignites,
The dance of life, it feels so right.

With laughter woven into grace,
In shadows, find the warm embrace.
For in each twist, a truth revealed,
The heart of light in darkness healed.

So let the rhythms guide my way,
In fractured forms, I choose to sway.
A tapestry of day and night,
We find ourselves in fractured light.

The Sweetness of Restoration

In gardens where the wildflowers bloom,
I find the strength to chase the gloom.
With every seed, a promise sown,
The sweetness of the life I've known.

Each petal holds a whisper true,
Of all the dreams that I pursue.
Restoration sings in vibrant hues,
A melody that life renews.

Through shifting sands and broken paths,
I gather joy from nature's baths.
With every breath, a healing thread,
A tapestry of life ahead.

In moments lost, I learn to see,
The beauty in tranquility.
From ashes rise, like phoenix flight,
In every ending, new delight.

I walk the trails of time and space,
Embracing every warm embrace.
The sweetest gift of life's embrace,
Is finding peace in every place.

In Search of Lost Fragments

I wander roads where memories fade,
In labyrinths of light and shade.
Each step a quest for what once was,
The echoes call, a silent buzz.

Through rusted gates and whispered lore,
I gather pieces from before.
In shadows deep, I seek to find,
The fragments left by heart and mind.

A song of loss, a hymn of gain,
In every tear, a pulse of rain.
With every turn, a tale unfurls,
Of dreams entwined in distant swirls.

I trace the lines of faded time,
In every pause, a quiet rhyme.
The puzzle speaks in colors bright,
As fragments merge to form the light.

In silent vows of love's intent,
I piece together what is meant.
For in the search, I find my way,
In lost fragments, bright as day.

Embracing the Full Spectrum of Self

In shadows and light, we find our grace,
Dancing through life, our true embrace.
Every flaw, a story, every scar, a gem,
In the tapestry woven, we are all the hem.

With vibrant colors, we paint our fate,
In the chaos of feelings, we cultivate.
Joy and sorrow, like rivers flow,
Together they weave the fabric we know.

Awakening whispers, through stillness we hear,
Acceptance becomes a soothing sphere.
The heart's open arms, a warm embrace,
In each moment we flourish, we find our place.

Like the sky adorned with stars at night,
So many versions, all shining bright.
To love every part, from shadow to light,
Is to embrace our journey, a powerful flight.

In the garden of self, we bloom and grow,
With patience and trust, we learn to glow.
For in the spectrum, we find our soul,
Embracing our wholeness, we become whole.

The Promise of Tomorrow's Wholeness

Each dawn brings whispers of dreams anew,
The sun rises softly, painting the view.
In the heartbeats of hope, we start to believe,
That tomorrow's embrace is what we can weave.

Through storms that have passed, we learn to stand,
Building resilience with a gentle hand.
Every challenge faced, a step on our way,
Towards the promise of brighter days.

The seeds we have sown in the soil of time,
Nurtured with love, they begin to climb.
Under moonlit skies, our visions take flight,
Carving our paths in the canvas of night.

Together we gather, united in song,
Believing as one, we will always belong.
A tapestry woven, threads intertwined,
The promise of wholeness, in each heart enshrined.

So let us march forth, with courage ablaze,
Embracing the journey, together we gaze.
For in every step, we find our release,
In tomorrow's wholeness, we discover peace.

Learning to Stand on Shattered Ground

Amidst the ruins, we find our feet,
In broken places, we gather the sweet.
Lessons embedded in fragments and scars,
Whispers of strength beneath the stars.

Each shard a reminder, a tale to be told,
In the heart of adversity, we grow bold.
Resilience blooms in the toughest of soil,
From the pain and the struggle, we learn to toil.

Learning to stand on this jagged terrain,
Nurturing courage from heartache and pain.
With every misstep, we gather our grace,
Finding our footing in a fragile space.

The cracks in our hearts let the light filter through,
In the depths of the struggle, we find what is true.
We rise from the ashes, renewed and refined,
On shattered ground, we no longer mind.

So here in the rubble, we carve out our song,
Finding the strength in where we belong.
With each step we take, we reclaim our sound,
Learning to stand on this shattered ground.

The Quest for Inner Unity

In the labyrinth of thoughts, we search and seek,
For unity within, in moments unique.
Voices of doubt may echo and call,
But we're on a quest, to rise above all.

Through valleys of silence, in stillness we plot,
Discovering fragments we thought we forgot.
The mind and the heart, where shadows convene,
We're stitching the pieces to make ourselves seen.

Embracing the duality, light meets the dark,
In each hidden corner, we find a spark.
Together they dance, a beautiful blend,
A harmony found as beginnings extend.

In the depths of our being, a treasure awaits,
Where love intertwines and compassion creates.
The quest for unity, a journey profound,
In the echoes of self, we're finally found.

With every deep breath, we weave a new thread,
In the fabric of life, where the lost are led.
A mosaic of moments, together in flow,
The quest for inner unity, forever we grow.

Journeying Toward Integration

Step by step, we walk this trail,
Searching for truth, where shadows pale.
With every heartbeat, we draw near,
Embracing each wound, shedding the fear.

Through valleys deep, and mountains high,
We dance with dreams beneath the sky.
In whispers soft, the lessons call,
Uniting our spirits, we rise, we fall.

With open hearts, we share the load,
Together we lighten the heaviest road.
In shared laughter, we find our way,
Connecting the pieces, come what may.

The journey flows like a river wide,
Carving our paths, as we abide.
In knowing the self, we find the whole,
As we rediscover our destined role.

Fragments of Renewal

In the quiet night, the stars ignite,
Shadows dance in luminous light.
Fragmented pieces, scattered afar,
Yearning to heal, like a distant star.

Through storms we weather, and rains we face,
We gather strength, in this sacred space.
Each broken shard, a story told,
In every fracture, a heart of gold.

With gentle hands, we shape anew,
Crafting our dreams from old to true.
Renewed in spirit, we take our stand,
A tapestry woven, designed by hand.

In whispers soft, a voice emerges,
Flowing like water, as life surges.
Each fragment shines, a path revealed,
In unity found, our fate is sealed.

In the Embrace of Wholeness

Upon the shore, where oceans meet,
We find our way, feel the heartbeat.
In the embrace of earth and sky,
We lift our eyes and learn to fly.

With open arms, we welcome change,
In every tide, we rearrange.
The pieces fit, as if by fate,
In harmony found, we celebrate.

Through every trial, we knit with care,
Building a bond that's rich and rare.
In laughter shared, in tears released,
Within this circle, our hearts find peace.

For in wholeness, the truth unfolds,
A story timeless that love beholds.
Together we stand, no fear to face,
In the embrace of everlasting grace.

Rebirth of the Unbroken

From ashes rise, the phoenix proud,
In silence found, amidst the crowd.
The spirit breathes, reborn in grace,
In each heartbeat, a shared embrace.

Forged in fire, we gather strength,
In vulnerability, we find our length.
The unbroken dance, with beauty rare,
In the tapestry of love, we dare.

With every sunrise, a canvas clean,
We paint our dreams in colors keen.
The shadows fade, in the golden light,
We walk our truth, prepared to fight.

Rebirth whispers, in every heart,
A journey anew, new paths to chart.
In the strength of souls, we grow anew,
Together, unbroken, we rise and pursue.

Rebuilding My Dreams

From ashes I rise, anew each day,
Gentle whispers guide my way.
With every step, I reclaim my light,
A tapestry of hopes, shining bright.

Brick by brick, I will construct,
A realm where fears are gently plucked.
With passion fierce, my spirit beams,
Embracing the journey, I rebuild my dreams.

Skies once gray, now painted blue,
Every challenge, a chance to renew.
In the dance of fate, I'll find my place,
A mosaic of joy, my heart will embrace.

Though shadows linger, I'll not retreat,
With every heartbeat, I'll find my beat.
The road ahead is paved with grace,
In the rebuilding, I find my space.

So here I stand, with dreams in hand,
Together, we rise, a united band.
The future calls, a bright sunrise,
In the rebirth, my spirit flies.

The Canvas of Autonomy

On a canvas blank, my spirit awaits,
Brush in hand, I create my fates.
Colors bold, patterns entwined,
A masterpiece born from a free mind.

With every stroke, my heart takes flight,
In the realm of choices, I find my light.
Each hue a story, a whisper of me,
A testament to who I can be.

In shadows and light, I find my form,
With gentle courage, I weather the storm.
No longer in chains, I boldly express,
Embracing my visions, I feel the finesse.

Choices abound, the world is wide,
In autonomy's grace, I take pride.
Dreams intertwined with passion's embrace,
On my canvas, I've found my place.

So here I paint, without fear or doubt,
Each stroke a declaration, inside and out.
In the art of living, I'll boldly create,
My canvas of autonomy, open the gate.

Sown Seeds of Self-Acceptance

In the garden of soul, I plant today,
Seeds of kindness, come what may.
With each breath, I nurture the ground,
Self-acceptance in silence found.

Roots dig deep, through heart and mind,
In the soil of love, treasures unwind.
Tending to wounds, I nurture the pain,
In the glow of hope, I'll rise again.

The blossoms emerge, petals unfurl,
Beauty in flaws, I give it a twirl.
Nature's design, unique in its grace,
Embracing my essence, I find my place.

Through storms and sunshine, I stand tall,
A garden resilient, I will not fall.
With every season, I grow and learn,
In self-acceptance, my spirit will burn.

So here I cultivate, with patience and love,
Sown seeds of growth, like stars above.
In the tapestry of life, I choose to thrive,
In this brilliant garden, I feel alive.

A Pilgrimage to Inner Peace

A journey unfolds, the path is clear,
In the quiet echo, I draw near.
With mindful steps, I wander low,
Each moment a treasure, a chance to grow.

The rustle of leaves, a calming song,
In the heart of nature, I belong.
With every breath, the burdens melt,
In the sacred stillness, a truth is felt.

Mountains may rise, rivers may bend,
In the search for peace, I'll never end.
With open eyes, the world reveals,
A sanctuary found in what it conceals.

Along this pilgrimage, I learn to see,
The beauty within, the light that's free.
In moments of silence, wisdom speaks,
In the journey's embrace, my spirit seeks.

So forward I go, with heart aglow,
Each step a blessing, a softened flow.
For in this quest, I've come to know,
Inner peace blooms as I let go.

Harmonies of the Heart's Reconstruction

In the silence where echoes dwell,
New chords of hope begin to swell.
Fragments of love, pieced with grace,
Creating a song in an open space.

Whispers of sorrow, soft and low,
Turn into melodies that gently flow.
Binding together the broken parts,
A symphony rises from healing hearts.

Each note a journey, every beat a sigh,
Resonating truths that never die.
In the rhythm of time, they find their place,
A dance of restoration, a warm embrace.

Bright harmonies spark the night,
Illuminating paths with their light.
Cradled by music, love's gentle art,
The heart finds strength, a brand new start.

In the stillness, hope takes flight,
Reconstruction through love's insight.
Together we rise, strong and free,
Harmonies guide, eternally.

Illuminated by the Light of Acceptance

In shadows deep, where doubts reside,
Acceptance shines, a radiant guide.
Flickers of grace, dispelling the dark,
Igniting the flame, igniting the spark.

With open hearts, we learn to see,
The beauty in flaw, the spirit in thee.
Casting aside what we cannot change,
Embracing the journey, profound and strange.

A soft light glows, where fear once stood,
Transforming the pain into something good.
Every scar tells a tale we share,
Illuminated truths, breathing the air.

In acceptance' arms, we find our way,
Guided by warmth, come what may.
Together we stand, though worlds may shift,
Illuminated hearts, the ultimate gift.

We rise as one, in unity's grace,
Finding our strength in every embrace.
In this light, we find our space,
Living with love, in the open place.

Finding Salvation in the Cracks

In the fractures where light seeps through,
Hope emerges, vibrant and new.
Hidden treasures in the broken seams,
Whispers of faith revive our dreams.

Searching for solace in jagged lines,
Revealing wisdom that brightly shines.
Salvation woven in the rough design,
Beauty found in life's intricate spine.

Each crack a story, each fissure a door,
Inviting us in to be so much more.
In the spaces where shadows play,
We find our peace, our guiding way.

Together we gather, heartbeats sync,
In the cracks, we bloom, begin to think.
The shattered pieces unveil a truth,
Resilience blooms in the heart of youth.

Through the gaps, we laugh and we cry,
Finding redemption as the moments fly.
In the cracks of time, our souls unite,
Step by step, into the light.

Awakening to Totality

In the stillness, the dawn breaks wide,
Awakening thoughts that no longer hide.
Whispers of knowledge, strong and clear,
Inviting the heart to cast off fear.

Moments converge, a seamless grace,
Heart and mind dance in a sacred place.
Awakening visions, vibrant and whole,
A tapestry woven, body and soul.

Through the chaos, clarity unfolds,
Secrets revealed, as the journey unfolds.
Each breath a promise, each step a choice,
In the sound of silence, we find our voice.

Embracing the wholeness, the joy, the pain,
Awakening truths like soft summer rain.
Totality sings in the light of the moon,
A symphony rising, a powerful tune.

Connected we stand, embracing the flow,
Awakening to all that we know.
In unity's embrace, we find our place,
Awakening to life, a beautiful grace.

Finding Strength in Solitude

In silence, I discover my core,
Whispers of strength I can't ignore.
Shadows linger, but light breaks through,
Solitude's gift shines bright and true.

A moment's pause, a breath, a thought,
In stillness, battles are bravely fought.
Each tear that falls, a lesson learned,
In solitude's fire, my spirit burned.

Mountains rise, yet I stand tall,
In my own heart, I hear the call.
Roots digging deep, I hold my ground,
In this quiet space, strength is found.

Voices fade, uncertainty reigns,
Yet in this calm, I break my chains.
With every heartbeat, hope ignites,
A warrior's spirit, ready for fights.

So here's to time spent all alone,
In solitude, I've truly grown.
For in the depths of my own mind,
A treasure of strength I seek to find.

The Tapestry of Transformation

Threads of change weave a design,
Stitch by stitch, my life aligns.
Colors fade and then revive,
In each transition, I feel alive.

Patterns shift, from dark to light,
Every struggle, a chance to fight.
In the loom of life, I find my place,
With every twist, a new embrace.

Past regrets may dim my view,
But hope's bright threads pull me through.
Each knot I tie, each tear I mend,
Crafting a story that knows no end.

Breaking free from what confounds,
In transformation, freedom pounds.
Embracing change, I learn to soar,
With open wings, I seek for more.

The tapestry grows, vibrant and bold,
In every corner, stories unfold.
A life reborn, a stunning sight,
In the fabric of change, I find my light.

Embracing Every Scar

Each scar whispers of battles fought,
Stories woven in every thought.
Marks of wisdom, not of shame,
Each flaw a part of my name.

Beneath the skin, treasures gleam,
Memories etched in every dream.
They tell of trials, of strength gained,
In every wound, my spirit remained.

Light dances on the paths I've walked,
In silent moments, I have mocked
The pain that shaped this heart of mine,
In every scar, resilience shines.

With open arms, I greet each line,
Each fracture forming a story divine.
In every mark, an essence lies,
A testament where courage flies.

So here I stand, proud and free,
Embracing scars that speak to me.
For in this journey, I'm not alone,
In every mark, I've found a home.

Blossoming from the Ruins

In shadows cast by what was lost,
New life emerges, regardless of cost.
Amidst the rubble, a seed takes flight,
From ashes born, it seeks the light.

Petals unfold, each hue a claim,
A vibrant dance of hope, not shame.
In barren ground, resilience thrives,
From brokenness, the spirit strives.

Rain may fall, but so does sun,
In every storm, I find the fun.
Nature's lesson, loud and clear,
In every ending, beginnings near.

Roots intertwine, embracing the past,
In every failure, strength amassed.
Blossoms rise where darkness dwelled,
In the heart of loss, beauty swelled.

So here I stand, blooming bright,
In the ruins, I find my light.
For from the ashes, I'll always grow,
A testament to life's gentle flow.

The Pulse of Resilience

In shadows deep, we find our light,
A trembling heart begins to fight.
Against the odds, we rise anew,
This pulse of strength flows deep and true.

With every fall, we learn to stand,
Each scar becomes a guiding hand.
Through stormy nights, we find our way,
A testament to brighter day.

In whispered dreams, our courage ignites,
Like stars that pierce the endless nights.
We forge ahead, with hope entwined,
A melody of grit combined.

Through trials faced, we stand as one,
The journey long, but never done.
With every breath, we cultivate,
The pulse of life that will not wait.

In hearts united, we embrace,
The stories shared, the dreams we chase.
For in our struggles, love will thrive,
This is the pulse that keeps us alive.

Awakening the Forgotten Self

In silent whispers of the past,
Memories linger, shadows cast.
Awake the soul that yearns to be,
Unveil the hidden tapestry.

Beneath the weight of time's embrace,
The fragments hide, yet hold their place.
With gentle hands, we stitch anew,
The stories lost, the dreams pursued.

In echoes soft, we hear the call,
A melody that breaks the fall.
Each note a step toward the light,
Awakening the inner might.

Through tangled paths of doubt and fear,
We rise to greet the voice we hear.
In every tear, a truth revealed,
The forgotten self, at last, unsealed.

With open hearts, we dance once more,
Embracing all that we explore.
Awakening, we find our grace,
The forgotten self embraces space.

Layers of Identity

In quiet depths, our essence lies,
Beneath the masks, the truth resides.
Each layer speaks of where we've been,
The stories woven, thick and thin.

With colors bright and shades so grey,
We paint our lives in grand array.
Yet underneath, the core remains,
A tapestry of joys and pains.

In every laugh, a history,
In every scar, a victory.
We peel the layers, one by one,
To find the heart that beats within.

Through storms we weather, bonds we weave,
In unity, we learn to grieve.
Together sharing all we've known,
The layers merged, the seeds we've sown.

In every moment, bold and true,
We claim our space, our rightful view.
For in our layers, we will see,
The rich mosaic of you and me.

Beneath the Surface

In tranquil depths, the waters hide,
A world beneath, where secrets bide.
With every ripple, tales unfold,
Of life and dreams both brave and bold.

Beneath the surface, currents flow,
The whispered truths we long to know.
In shadows deep, where silence reigns,
The heart's desire, the soul's remains.

Yet in the depths, there's beauty found,
In hidden realms, where hope is crowned.
The vibrant life that thrives unseen,
A dance of light in shades of green.

With courage, we dive beyond the veil,
To face the fears, to sail the gale.
For in the depths, we find our grace,
An ancient wisdom we embrace.

Beneath the surface, we emerge,
With open hearts, our spirits surge.
For every layer peeled away,
Reveals the dawn of a brighter day.

I Rise

From ashes cold, I find my spark,
In darkest nights, I light the dark.
With every bruise, I learn to soar,
A phoenix bold, I will restore.

Through trials faced, I claim my ground,
In whispered strength, my voice resounds.
No chains can bind this heart of fire,
For in my soul, I find desire.

Each wound a story, each tear a guide,
In every fall, I choose to ride.
With every breath, I break the mold,
In strength and grace, my spirit bold.

Through storm and calm, I navigate,
With open heart, I cultivate.
For in my rise, the world may see,
The power born from deep within me.

I rise, I shine, I stand anew,
With every dawn, I am pulled through.
For in this journey, I embrace,
The light that lives in every space.

Stitched Together by Time

In the fabric of days gone past,
Threads entwine, a tapestry vast.
Moments stitched with care and grace,
Time weaves us through every space.

Memories flutter like leaves in breeze,
Marked by joy and pain that frees.
Each seam a tale, each stitch a sigh,
Binding hearts that refuse to cry.

Whispers of laughter echo still,
In the quilt of life, we find our will.
Colors blend from dusk to dawn,
Hope is the thread we're woven on.

Through the years, we dance and twine,
Beneath the stars, we boldly shine.
Together, we embrace the flow,
Stitched by time, forever aglow.

In twilight's hue, our shadows cast,
Linked by moments that forever last.
We rise anew as seasons change,
In the art of love, we're not estranged.

Unfolding in the Light of Acceptance

With open arms, we seek the sun,
Embracing all, the lost, the won.
Each flaw, a note in our sweet song,
In acceptance, we find where we belong.

Shadows fade in the dawning glow,
As we learn to let our true selves show.
Every scar tells a story clear,
In the light of love, we cast out fear.

Breath by breath, we shed the weight,
Discovering paths that we create.
In each moment, a chance to grow,
In the gentle light, we come to know.

With every dawn, we rise anew,
In the soft embrace of skies so blue.
Together, we weave a brighter way,
In acceptance, we find our stay.

Every heart is a field to tend,
Roots entwined, we learn to mend.
In this garden of our own design,
Unfolding softly, a love divine.

A Garden of Reclaimed Dreams

Once buried deep beneath the earth,
Seeds of hope await rebirth.
In the soil of time, they stretch and bloom,
Painting visions, dispelling gloom.

Follow the whispers of gentle hearts,
For each new journey, a fresh start.
Tending to dreams with love and care,
A vibrant tapestry we proudly share.

Petals open, colors ignite,
Every wish takes its rightful flight.
The fragrance of courage fills the air,
In this garden, we learn to dare.

Wildflowers dance in the softest breeze,
In their beauty, we find our ease.
Each moment becomes vivid and true,
As reclamation shapes me and you.

Under the sun's warm, golden beams,
We gather the remnants of scattered dreams.
With every blossom, we cheer and sing,
In this garden, our souls take wing.

The Heart's Quiet Healing

In the hushed stillness, whispers flow,
Healing begins when we learn to slow.
Each heartbeat echoes soft and clear,
In the silence, we draw near.

Gentle waves upon the shore,
Wash away what was held before.
With every breath, we start anew,
In the quiet, love breaks through.

Time draws circles, spaces to mend,
In our hearts, we find a friend.
Patience blooms like a tender flower,
In stillness, we reclaim our power.

Through tender moments, shadows fade,
We plant seeds of hope, unafraid.
Listen closely to the song inside,
In the heart's quiet, we abide.

Healing journeys twist and turn,
In every scar, there's more to learn.
With open hearts, we face the dawn,
In gentle healing, we carry on.

The Fire of Rejuvenation

In the heart where ashes lay,
New flames flicker, dance, and sway.
From the warmth of yesterday,
Life ignites, brightens the gray.

Old scars whisper tales of strife,
Yet in their midst, blooms new life.
With each spark, the spirit soars,
A phoenix rising, love restores.

Embers hold the promise true,
Of beginnings born anew.
In the blaze, we shed the past,
Finding strength, we'll stand steadfast.

With every heartbeat, fire grows,
Filling souls with vibrant glow.
We rise together, hand in hand,
Rejuvenated, we take a stand.

Through the flames, we are reborn,
Out of shadow, into dawn.
In our hearts, the fire gleams,
Breathing hope, igniting dreams.

Lighthouse in the Storm

When dark clouds gather above,
A beacon shines, a symbol of love.
Its light cuts through night's despair,
Guiding lost hearts with tender care.

Waves crash hard against the shore,
But the lighthouse stands evermore.
With strength that defies the tide,
It whispers hope, a faithful guide.

In swirling winds, courage wakes,
An anchor when the heart aches.
Through tempests fierce and wild roar,
The light remains, a steadfast core.

Each pulse, a promise to hold tight,
Through darkest days, we find our light.
The storm may rage, the night may loom,
But faith will guide us through the gloom.

On paths untraveled, shadows play,
Yet the lighthouse guides the way.
With every flicker, hope is born,
In the storm, we find our dawn.

Shattered No More

Broken pieces on the floor,
Reflecting dreams we can restore.
In the silence, strength unfolds,
From the shards, new stories told.

With gentle care, we start anew,
Crafting beauty from the blue.
Each fracture tells a tale of grace,
In the cracks, we find our place.

Hands embraced in tender grace,
Healing wounds we now embrace.
What was lost begins to soar,
Together, we are shattered no more.

With every dawn, a chance to mend,
We rise from ashes, hearts ascend.
Gathered fragments, bright and true,
In unity, we break right through.

Once lost, now whole we stand tall,
Each journey shapes us through it all.
No longer broken, hearts in bloom,
Together, we dispel the gloom.

The Mosaic of Resilience

A canvas wild with hues of pain,
Each fragment tells of loss and gain.
In chaos, beauty finds a way,
Colors blend in bright display.

Though storms may shake, we hold our ground,
In unity, our strength resounds.
Each piece a tale, a journey's stride,
In every crack, our dreams abide.

The shards of past now shine so bright,
Reflecting hope, igniting light.
From trials faced, we gather grace,
In resilience, we find our place.

Together, we create a whole,
Mosaic formed with every soul.
With colors rich and textures bold,
We share our stories, hearts unfold.

Through time's embrace, we'll stand as one,
With every moment, new life begun.
In life's vast tapestry we weave,
A mosaic born of love, believe.